Overcoming the Enemy's Plan II

AN ANTHOLOGY

TENITA C. JOHNSON

Published by So It Is Written, LLC
Detroit, MI
SoItIsWritten.net

Overcoming the Enemy's Plan II: An Anthology

Edited by: So It Is Written – www.SoItIsWritten.net

Formatting: Ya Ya Ya Creative – YaYaYaCreative@gmail.com

ISBN: 979-8-9912588-3-8

LCCN: 2024921340

PRINTED AND BOUND IN THE UNITED STATES OF AMERICA

TABLE OF CONTENTS

FOREWORD

Prophetess Shawndra C. Johnson

 Have you ever felt like you were on the brink of something great? Something you *know* God created you to do?

However, there seems to be one problem: The devil has been hot on your tracks and just won't leave you alone! Instead of being excited about your calling, you are worried and doubtful. You even wonder if you heard God call your name at all!

Good news! (I heard you say, "Did she just say good news?") Yes! I said it, and I meant it. The good news is that your blessings and breakthroughs are at hand. You can feel it. But the devil knows it, too. He wants to do everything he can to thwart your destiny. What the enemy meant for evil God can, and will, turn it around for your good. He is going to make it work in your favor and give you double for your trouble.

You were never left alone. You weren't confused. There is nothing wrong with your hearing. You heard Him correctly.

It's just that the enemy heard Him, too. You are going to turn the world on its axis despite the opposition. Hold your head up high! Keep moving forward! Stand flat-footed and declare the Word of the Lord! Don't look back now because your mind-blowing destiny and blessings have arrived.

Congratulations! You have officially *Overcome the Enemy's Plan*!

BEAUTY IN BROKENNESS

Dr. Ashley Tauriac

"Sure! I can move your car for you. Where is it parked and where are your keys?"

I blinked, confused for a second. I thought I was only tired, and it would come back to me after I processed for a bit.

"I drove my car to go to the medical student clinic and" *Nothing.* I couldn't remember anything else.

I replied, "I don't know."

Honestly, I can't remember the exchange at all. In fact, the last thing I remember was the doctor telling me that I needed to go to the ER to get evaluated. That was on May 18th. The next thing I remember was waking up in a hospital bed and reading a sign that said, "Today is May 25."

That was the beginning of my diagnosis, and the journey through the aftermath, of bacterial meningitis. Four days after graduating from medical school, I was admitted to the hospital with a severe infection of the brain. During my hospital stay, I experienced trouble communicating, memory problems, swelling in the brain, and a collapsed lung. I don't remember most of that though. I'm told I was combative, angry and illogical, which is quite different from my normal personality. Despite the many complications, three weeks later, I was slowly improving and, according to everyone around me, I was getting back to my normal self. Everyone told me I should be fine to begin my residency only a month after leaving the hospital. No one seemed to have any serious concerns . . . except *me*.

I couldn't remember much of anything about the entire month of May. Friends came to visit and talked about our graduation from medical school, which had taken place just before I was admitted to the hospital. It was a huge day with friends and family galore. It was a wonderful week of celebrating. It was the biggest accomplishment of my life, but I couldn't remember anything about it. I didn't even believe that I was there until I saw pictures of myself there. Two days after I was discharged from the hospital, I had a follow-up appointment with the doctor, who had also seen me daily during my hospital stay. I didn't recognize him at all. In addition, I was exhausted. I slept about sixteen hours a day the first few weeks out of the hospital. I also got tired simply trying to eat a meal.

I seemed to be healing much slower than predicted and much slower than I expected. But other than the gaps in my memory and the utter exhaustion, life was fairly normal. I could continue

I knew God to be a loving, caring Father who could do miracles and change the very fabric of life.

mostly normal conversations and answer questions. I finished doing all the paperwork I needed to start my residency, and everything looked like it was going to be fine.

Up until then, my life had honestly been really good. I grew up in church and went to a Christian school as a child. I was absolutely in love with God. I knew all about the classic biblical stories. I knew God to be a loving, caring Father who could do miracles and change the very fabric of life. The only real stressors I had lived through were my parents' divorce and grandfather's illness and death. My church lined up missionaries and pastors who recounted that God was the same yesterday, today and forever. I prayed for God to show up like the God of the Bible and to do incredible things in my life, as well.

See, one thing we don't realize about praying for miracles is that we have to be placed in circumstances that require a miracle. Basically, God doesn't usually intervene in regular days and make them spectacular just for fun; He intervenes in horrible days and uses them to remind us of who He truly is. Meningitis became the circumstance I didn't realize I needed to truly see God and myself clearer than I ever had before.

After battling meningitis, I was initially fine spiritually. I knew God would never leave me or forsake me. I knew so many biblical stories of how God healed, changed circumstances, and recovered and redeemed things that were lost. I knew I had a clear word from God that I was going to be a doctor, and I was willing to wait for Him to show up and completely heal and restore me.

The faith I started with began to wane as things grew increasingly more difficult.

But as the months and prayers rolled on, complete healing was not a part of my journey. I never received a single, momentary completeness that returned me to my former faith-filled, confident, well-spoken academic self. The faith I started with began to wane as things grew increasingly more difficult.

I was eventually pulled off work and referred for cognitive testing and counseling for depression. Because I had just started to work as a doctor, I was no longer receiving a paycheck, and I wasn't eligible for FMLA or unemployment benefits. The cognitive testing that was supposed to clear me to return to work was pushed back weeks as I awaited my new employer's medical insurance to officially begin.

I literally felt like an imposter in my own body. Formerly easy things, like spelling my own name or writing my phone number correctly, I got wrong time after time. More than anything, I worried constantly whether the eight years and hundreds of thousands of dollars I had just invested in school were going down the drain and I would never be able to work as a doctor again.

But God . . .

God brought back Scriptures from my Christian school days where we were regularly challenged, almost daily, to commit them to memory. God revealed to me how much I defined myself by my abilities. I was known for being able to do anything and everything well, and I felt I had lost it all. Therefore, I felt like I lost me. But God lovingly and patiently reminded me, *"Though the mountains be shaken and the hill be removed, yet my unfailing love for you will not be shaken nor my covenant of peace be removed," says the Lord, who has compassion on you* (Isaiah 54:9-11).

He reminded me that, as a Christian, my identity doesn't lie in what I can do well or how much I have accomplished. Come sickness, financial strain, unclear direction in life, disappointments, or fear that our lives are crumbling; at the end of the day, life is secure when we are defined by God only. If we're standing strong in only Him, we'll barely notice when everything else fails. *Therefore, since we are receiving a kingdom that cannot be shaken, let us be thankful* (Hebrews 12:28a).

A few weeks later, I was cleared to return to work and began my intern year. I was thankful that even if God didn't heal me in the way I wanted, He still continued to encourage me in my recovery. I returned to work with lots of Bible verses, a decreased schedule, and close monitoring from the hospital staff. I worked hard with help from speech therapy, my doctor, and my counselor to implement workarounds in my day and accommodations for my slower processing ability. I arrived to work an hour before everyone else, so I had time to re-check my work. As my schedule would allow, I took a nap every day and slept eight hours every night. But the practical accommodation didn't overcome the emotional ones I had to deal with that year.

My residency was in general pediatrics. That meant that as I returned to full-time work, I was working 80+ hours a week with sick children. Somewhere between the patients' struggles and my own, I started to question God again.

Medicine has come a long way in the last hundred years, but there are still countless problems we just cannot fix. I started to see my job as a place where I went to work to pretend to help people; but instead, I just watched children suffer and/or die. I couldn't stomach the injustice I was seeing and our inability to fix so many problems. We saw obvious signs of child abuse, but then we were unable to prove it. We had to send the child home with the family, terrified they'd be back in worse shape later. One baby returned after child abuse, completely paralyzed from the neck-down, after being shaken so hard because he wouldn't stop crying. All the medicine in the world couldn't reverse the amount of life-altering damage that was done to him. All the best medication in the world couldn't fix the metastatic cancer the teenager faced—not only on her way to death—but also in the insufferable pain that made her cry all day long. All the medicine in the world hadn't saved me from the cognitive impairment, the medical bills, the insecurity, and instability I experienced.

I questioned the very faith I had depended on for so long. Why did God put us here on earth just to suffer?

With all the pain, and all the suffering, and all the struggles that life here on earth brings, what is the point of our actual lives?

If medicine couldn't really fix things, and it was going to be this difficult, maybe I should just give up and walk away.

I questioned the very faith I had depended on for so long. Why did God put us here on earth just to suffer? Why don't Christians pray a prayer of salvation, and then literally go immediately to Heaven? The hospital felt like a place where God put all of the people that He didn't care enough about to help them anymore.

Around that time, I started going through the plan of redemption with a pastor from church. This is also known as the Redemption Mandate. We looked at the story that the Bible as a whole tells, instead of simply the individual stories we often concentrate on in church. The Bible details a story of God creating people to live on earth and emulate Himself. He started with designing and creating the world, then entrusting it to humans. His plan was that we would walk with Him, using His ideas and our abilities to further develop the world. When sin entered the picture, the world and the work we did was cursed and made more difficult, but not destroyed. The plan was more challenging, but not impossible.

We were to use the gifts God gave us to take care of the world in His way. Whether it's farming, medicine, technology, ministry or anything else, God's plan was that we would take those things that had been destroyed by sin and cursed on the earth and do our best to improve and advance the world. The story of God's redemption plays out repeatedly through the Scriptures, including God liberating Israel from Egypt and providing social, psychological, financial, and political healing through his miracles. We see it in the stories of Jesus healing people from pain, demons, illness and religious confusion. He healed them from anything that would hinder their ability to hear God and walk out their calling on earth. Then, we see God leave the task of sharing His plan of redemption—not only of souls— but also of this earth to the Christian church. In the New

Testament, He encourages us to go into all the world, teaching them all that God has taught us.

Sometimes the biblical story is simply taught as a call to believe in God and get saved. But if part of God's plan is that we also take care of the earth He painstakingly created and entrusted to us, then our jobs outside of the church really matter. We aren't all called to full-time ministry for a reason. I realized then, that despite the pain, the suffering, and the inability of medicine to fix so many problems, God had specifically called me to be a doctor. He called me to use the skills He has entrusted me with to go into the world and do my part in sharing His plan of redemption of souls and of this earth. Being a Christian in the workplace affords me the opportunity to provide something beautiful: a hope and an eternal healing for my patients, even when the medications and treatments don't work, and my plans don't go as I had hoped.

As I continued my studies with our pastor, I discovered that redemption was only half of the story. I was overlooking a major chapter as I walked out God's calling on my life: that of *relationships*.

I tried to maintain relationships with friends throughout my residency. But with my work schedule, and the extra hours I had to devote to rest because of my illness, there were just not enough hours in the day. Additionally, it turns out that I had somehow offended some friends and family with things I had said while still actively sick. I found myself trying to repair relationships that I couldn't recall destroying. In turn, some of my medical friends were more annoyed than supportive as I had to continue to ask for accommodation at work.

"I wish I could sleep eleven hours a day," one other resident told me. This person didn't realize that the only way I pulled that off was by skipping meals and everything else except work. I felt a growing strain in my relationships with friends and family. They had the same disappointment in me that I had in myself. I felt like they saw me as all that I had been reduced to a complaining workaholic who couldn't see anything positive anymore.

I lost a lot of friendships that year. The majority of those friends were other Christians who kept telling me to just pull myself together and find my joy in God. Even my medical colleagues shrugged off my continual struggles with cognitive impairment. They said I was just exaggerating. I often felt like I was standing in the middle of a room screaming, but everyone just kept walking by, saying, "You look fine to me!"

> *But somehow, at the bottom of the barrel, I found the One who mattered the most. Through it all, God let me mourn all the horrible losses that year.*

My counselor ended our sessions, saying I was too depressed, and she couldn't help me anymore. It seemed like I had no one left. But somehow, at the bottom of the barrel, I found the One who mattered the most. Through it all, God let me mourn all the horrible losses that year. He let me sob daily for months on end, without growing tired or giving up on me. He let me be imperfect, broken, harsh and ugly, and somehow, continued to love me through the difficulties of that year.

Months in, I had an extra shift at the hospital in the emergency department. I spent a grueling day trying to stabilize a young girl who had attempted suicide. She had taken a massive number of pills that caused a host of medical complications, but not actual death as she had intended. We involved consult after consult, trying to stabilize her. We also had to work out a plan on how to get her emotionally stable. I went home, exhausted, sitting on the floor next to the bed as I normally did when I got home. I was prepared to sob another night away.

But this particular time, something new took over. I started recounting the overwhelming year I had just had, and how much I felt abandoned. If this was what the rest of my life was going to be, I couldn't see how it could be worth it. I thought back to the patient from earlier, who had taken a handful of pills to end her life. I realized that she didn't know how to do it correctly because she didn't have enough medical knowledge of what would actually happen. But I knew what she had done wrong.

More than that, I knew exactly what I needed to take in order to do it correctly.

I went to the cabinet and got the pills and a bottle of water. But somehow, I couldn't move my hand up to my mouth; something invisible, yet firm, held it on my lap. Then I heard God say, "This doesn't sound like something you would do." He stopped me from making the worst mistakes in the worst of years, and I can't thank Him enough for doing so.

But God doesn't offer love to us because of the things we do well. He offers us love regardless of what we give back to Him.

God later told me, "Those days you cried were my favorites."

I thought that was harsh because those days were my nightmares for me. They were signs of me being unable to put back together things like I always had; they were signs of my brokenness. But God said, "They were just you being honest and bringing yourself to me. I love you more than anything else."

I physically could not give Him anything worth having, but broken, confused and angry me. He accepted me as is and still said He loved me. I started to understand love in a completely new way that year. Up until then, love and acceptance seemed like a reward for me performing perfectly and impressing everyone. But when the ability to impress everyone went away, I assumed love would, too, especially as I watched many of my relationships collapse. But God doesn't offer love to us because of the things we do well. He offers us love regardless of what we give back to Him. Taking perfection out of the equation entirely allowed me to see the complete, whole and beautiful aspect of God's love so much clearer.

But even more incredibly, you would think that our own brokenness left us completely worthless of accomplishing anything. With the huge task God left of us taking care of the world, it seems like our incompleteness and imperfections would make that an impossible task. How could imperfect people ever accomplish anything worthwhile? But as the year went on, God gave me the ability to help patients, repair relationships, and He even healed my own heart. He took my limited abilities, which should have left me and my life worthless, and somehow was able to do perfect things in spite of my limitations. I kept double- and triple-checking my work, terrified and aware that my writing a decimal point out of place could literally kill a patient. However, nothing like that ever happened. Instead, I had a growing list of incredible patient encounters, words of knowledge, and beautiful stories with coworkers that reminded me again that God was never afraid of my limitations, even if I was.

Brokenness only equals perfection if it includes God. The Word of God in 2 Corinthians 12:8-10 describes Paul asking God to take away a struggle of his.

Three times I pleaded with the Lord to take it away from me. But He said to me, "My grace is sufficient for you, for my power is made perfect in weakness." Therefore, I will boast all the more gladly about my weaknesses, so that Christ's power may rest on me. That's why, for Christ's sake, I delight in weaknesses, insults, hardships, in persecutions, in difficulties. For when I am weak, then I am strong.

God doesn't ask us to bring perfection in order to be loved. He simply asks us to bring ourselves, and He perfects the rest.

One day, I caught up with my friend who I hadn't seen in while. This friend took care of my car the day I was admitted to the hospital for meningitis. She said that day, I looked extremely ill, and I wasn't able to tell her where the car was. After much searching, she found it parked erratically outside of the student health clinic in a 15-minute parking spot. The front driver's side door was wide open, and my purse and keys were sitting on the front seat. Yet, after sitting there for hours, somehow, it was undisturbed. No parking tickets. No stolen items. No stolen car. That car reminded me that God was involved from the very beginning. He may not have kept me from getting sick, but He kept me from death and life-long injury. He may not have fixed every problem I encountered that year, but He protected things like my car, my job, and my sanity in a situation where I would have lost all of them.

He may not have kept me from all that went wrong, but He held my hand through every rough day and never gave up on me, even when I wanted to give up on Him. Most amazing, He helped me every day to do a job I shouldn't have been able to do.

I completed my residency training three years later and saw the miracle it was for the girl with a brain injury to finish her training with no patients lost, no lawsuits filed, no injuries done, and no mistakes made.

God worked in my brokenness, reminding me constantly that with and through Him, I can achieve so much more than I ever thought possible. Don't forget. He's still there, both on my side and on yours. Regardless of how bleak the situation may be, He will never let you go.

Reflection Questions

1. What does it take to dream like God instead of dreaming like the world?

   _____

   _____

   _____

   _____

2. How do you get to the source of a problem in your life, and let God change your heart first, and your actions later?

   _____

   _____

   _____

   _____

3. *What would it look like to apply the cross to your biggest problem right now?*

_____

_____

_____

_____

4. *Are you confident in who you are and in what God can do in your life in spite of your imperfections? What would it take to change your perception of self?*

_____

_____

_____

_____

ABOUT THE AUTHOR

Dr. Ashley Tauriac

Dr. Ashley Tauriac has focused for the last fifteen years on teaching and studying concepts concerning faith at work. After finishing her medical training at Vanderbilt, she worked for several years part-time as a pediatrician, and part-time for her church, planning international medical mission trips. Currently, as a physician, she works with newborns and teaches at the local medical school. She's from New Mexico, even though she has been living in Nashville for the last twenty years. She loves movies, music, dancing and encouraging friends to discover and grow in their God-given purpose.

BROKEN TO BLESSED
MY HEALING JOURNEY

Nicole D. Shepherd

Dreams & Revelations

I had a dream that I was in a canoe in a large body of water. The canoe surprised me because it was too small compared to the amount of water it was sitting in. I was in the canoe with one of my favorite characters from *Grey's Anatomy*, Arizona Roberts. The character's personality is very bubbly, friendly and optimistic. She smiled at me as we sat in the canoe, which was right at the shore. I looked out at the large body of water and felt a little overwhelmed and apprehensive; yet, I felt peaceful at the same time.

Later, I understood why that part of the dream was significant. The dream shifted. I was in my childhood home, except the house was in disarray. The house looked as if someone broke in and ransacked it. Furniture was thrown around and flipped over. There was broken wood hanging from the ceiling. I was standing in what was the breakfast nook. The floor was covered with water throughout the house. I was looking at the house my family and I grew up in, but didn't recognize the interior of the house. The house I grew up in was neat, clean and well put together. Many times, I have a dream, and God will give me interpretation while I am

Many times, I have a dream, and God will give me interpretation while I am still dreaming.

still dreaming. That was not the case this time. I did not understand what the dream meant. I knew I needed to seek the Lord for revelation and understanding.

I woke up from the dream and went right into prayer. I asked God what the dream meant. Why was I dreaming about my childhood home? Why did it look so different than it did when I was growing up? Why was the house in my dream so dark and cold when the house I grew up in (in real life) was warm and inviting? I didn't understand what a character from *Grey's Anatomy* was doing in my dream. What did Arizona Roberts have to do with my childhood?

The Holy Spirit revealed to me that the house represented *me*. I was broken and had been since I was a child. On the outside, I looked like any other person. I did not look like what I felt inside. I appeared to have it all together on the outside. But what was going on internally was a different story, a different battle, that no one knew about.

Hidden Pain & Unseen Battles

As a child, a friend's sister molested me. I held the secret until I was an adult. I hid the hurt and confusion deep inside, and I tried to keep it buried. I was afraid that I would be in trouble if I told my parents. I was terrified whenever I saw her, which was not often. She lived on the east side of Detroit, and I lived on the west side. I was also molested by my father's "friend." Once when he visited with my father, he thought I was asleep. He came into my room and kissed my neck before touching me inappropriately.

I froze.

I was terrified of what would happen if he knew I was awake. I was terrified of what he would do if I continued to pretend to be asleep. I didn't know how my father would react if I told him that his friend, who, like my father, was a police officer, was molesting me. I felt like because this happened to me as a young child, I shouldn't be surprised that it happened again. I figured I wasn't worth anything. I could not tell anyone that I was walking around feeling like I was nothing. I disguised my low self-esteem with what I thought confidence looked like. I tried to look like and act like people who I thought exuded confidence. All the while, I felt like I did not deserve to live. I accepted Christ at the age of seven, but no one taught me about spiritual matters. I thought that God was disappointed in me, even though I was a child and could not control any of the aforementioned situations.

It was not until my older sister began having Bible study out of her home that I shared with her that I had been molested by our father's friend. I don't believe I ever told anyone about being molested by our friend's older sister. My parents both passed, not knowing what happened to me. I carried the weight of the guilt, as if it were *my* fault. At the time, I didn't understand the spiritual ramifications of what took place.

I didn't know that I had been exposed to a spirit of perversion. I didn't know that a spirit of perversion comes with a spirit of lust and several other unclean spirits. I also carried a spirit of shame and guilt.

I continued to live my life as normally as I could. I have married and divorced multiple times. I never asked God to lead me in my marriages. I didn't make Christ Lord over my relationships. I have experienced emotional abuse, verbal abuse and physical abuse. I have been in relationships where I was so torn down that I believed I could walk the streets completely naked, and no one would notice me. Surely, this was because I thought I was worth nothing. I fought back, but I didn't know how the words that were spoken to me or yelled at me

I was in and out of church as a teenager. ... I lived how I wanted, without regard for God.

by my husband left deeper scars than the black eye or the physical scars from forced sex. I didn't know that I would carry those words with me for far longer than I carried the embarrassment of getting into physical fights with my husband in public. I didn't understand how the impact of trauma from molestation would guide decisions I made as an adult.

I was in and out of church as a teenager. I was not trying to live a holy life. I believed in God, but I didn't have a relationship with Him, nor did I know it was even possible. I lived how I wanted, without regard for God. I was guilty of fornication and adultery. I believed that God didn't care about me because of my past experiences. I remarried, still carrying baggage from my first marriage and my childhood. We struggled financially. He didn't want me to work, nor did he keep a job. He decided to sell drugs out of our apartment. I had never been around drugs and all that brought with it. I was against it, but he brought drugs to our home anyway. I left with my two children while I was pregnant with my third, with nowhere to go.

Seeking Refuge & Finding Peace

I went to the police department for help, and they drove me to a homeless shelter. I remember the intake process consisted of several questions. They took us to a room that had a twin bed and a bunk bed. I was grateful that we were in a room alone. Once we were left in the room, I put my children to bed and laid down myself. I felt like I had hit rock bottom. *How could I allow myself to be in this situation with my babies!* I felt unworthy to be called anyone's mother. I buried my head in the pillow while I cried so my babies couldn't hear me. As I lay there, it felt like my mind opened and in poured peace. I was able to fall asleep.

The next morning, I woke up feeling like there was nowhere to go from there, except *up*.

Weeks later, I gave birth to my third child. I was able to return home to my childhood home. I experienced post-partum depression. I couldn't even get out of bed to pick my newborn baby up. I lay there, unable to soothe her because I felt worthless. I was a married woman, separated from my husband with three children to take care of by myself. My sister pulled me out of bed, dressed me and put make-up on my face. What may seem like a small thing to some was something that rescued me from being overtaken by a spirit of depression.

I reconciled with my second husband. He decided we would move to California. We packed up our apartment. He rented a car and drove to California. He promised he would send for me later. Once I arrived in California, he took me to a hotel that included a kitchenette. We did not unpack the car, which contained all our luggage. The next morning, the rental car was missing. What I thought was a theft turned out to be the rental car company retrieving their rental. My husband was supposed to return the car but did not.

I was in California with my youngest child, with no clothes for either of us. There was a knock on the door. I opened the door to find the police there to arrest him. *What was I to do now?* I was alone in California with my daughter, who was four years old. I had no job or contacts. No family or resources. I couldn't pay for the hotel, so we had to leave. I didn't know what to do, so I walked into another hotel during breakfast to act as though we had a room there to feed my daughter. I called a friend back home who invited me to come stay with her. I had no way to get home, though. All I had was a cell phone that was running out of minutes. Somehow, my husband was released from jail. But, by that point, I told him I was leaving to go back to Michigan.

Back home in Detroit, I moved in with a close friend and her children. We navigated the hardships of single parenthood, supporting each other emotionally and financially. We pooled resources and shared responsibilities, which made the burdens a bit more bearable. I secured a job, and, with careful planning, I saved enough money to rent a one-bedroom apartment. I didn't care that the space in my apartment was small; I was overjoyed by the fact that I had all three of my children with me under one roof. Despite these strides, life remained a constant struggle. Financial pressures, emotional turmoil, and the daily demands of raising

I repeatedly found myself in relationships that mirrored my internal chaos.

children took a toll. I was living life on my own terms; yet my choices in relationships revealed a different truth. I had unresolved pain and a deep-seated need for connection. I repeatedly found myself in relationships that mirrored my internal chaos. Each relationship reflected my unhealed wounds, chosen from a place of brokenness rather than a place of healing.

Unbeknownst to me, I had never truly confronted the trauma of my past. The scars of previous experiences lingered, influencing my decisions and interactions. I carried this baggage into every romantic relationship, often sabotaging it with my unresolved issues. The cycle of seeking love and comfort in others, without first healing myself, perpetuated my suffering. It was clear that until I faced my trauma head-on, I would continue to re-live it in various forms.

I continued to live my life not concerned about God. I eventually found myself considering what my children's life would be like if I were not alive. It crossed my mind that my children might be better off without me. The weight of this thought filled my mind with despair. Again, I lay in bed muffling my cries on the pillow. I was trapped in thoughts of hopelessness and self-doubt. I was in a dark space, and I didn't know how to get out. How could I guide my children to make better decisions when I couldn't trust myself to make wise decisions?

In my lowest moment, I found myself praying to God, asking Him to take my life— much like the prophet Elijah when he was hiding in the cave. The emotional pain felt unbearable, and the shame of my failures was overwhelming.

A Path to Healing and Redemption

As the tears flowed, I was suddenly overcome by a sensation of peace, much like the peace I experienced in the shelter. The peace washed all over me. I didn't understand what was happening or why. But in that moment, the chaos in my mind was quieted. The storm that was raging inside of me subsided and was replaced by a sense of calm. I didn't know at the time that it was God giving me peace that surpassed my understanding,

The unexpected peace gave me a significant shift in my perspective. The next morning, I found the resolve to get out of bed and face the day. I tried to hide my pain from my children. I struggled financially. I made games out of my struggle. I had tea parties on a blanket spread out on the floor with my babies that consisted of potato chips and iced tea because that was all I had. It was all I could do to make things fun. I needed a better way to provide for my children, so I went to nursing school.

I was beginning to find my footing finally ... or so I thought.

Suddenly, my grandmother passed away. During her home-going service, people were praising God and dancing unto the Lord. A woman who I did not know came over to me and told me that my life was about to change. I didn't

> *It was at that moment that I realized that she couldn't accomplish those things on her own. I knew it had to be God.*

know what to do with that information. I had never received a prophetic word, nor did I know what a prophecy was. She invited me up to the altar to dance with everyone else. I declined.

Empowerment & New Beginnings

During orientation for my job at a new nursing facility, I met a nurse who was talking about starting an assisted living home. I was intrigued. She asked me if I went to church, and I said, "No." She asked me if I wanted to listen to a CD from her church. I attempted to listen, but I was turned off by the music. I thought it was only supposed to be a message. I continued to talk with her at work. She shared with me her progress in starting her business. I noticed how things were moving in her life. Instead of getting one house, she opened two assisted living homes. It was at that moment that I realized that she couldn't accomplish those things on her own. I knew it had to be God.

I decided to visit her church. One of my daughters went with me. During that service, the pastor talked about some of the things I was just talking about at home in random conversations. There was no way possible for this to be, except God heard me. I don't know what the entire message was about because I was amazed by the fact that God heard me.

I reconnected with a friend from my past. We talked on the phone and agreed to see each other. He came to my apartment, which was now a two-bedroom apartment in a much better complex. He asked to borrow my iPod because he was leaving town later that week for a trip. He told me that he would call me when he returned. A couple of weeks passed. While I was at work, he called me and told me that he had just been released from jail. He said that he was accused of molesting his niece. I couldn't believe it! Even with my past experiences, I couldn't believe that he was capable of such horrible actions. I stood by his side during his court appearances. I believed he was innocent. He pleaded guilty so that he could do the two years his court-appointed lawyer told him he would have to do. He was placed in custody and taken to prison. I continued to support him despite his prison sentence. I was there for him emotionally and financially. Our friendship grew from just friends to feelings of love for each other.

We were married while he was still in prison.

I continued to go to church. During the offering, the pastor released prophetic words and laid hands upon people. I had never witnessed any of these things. My daughter asked me if we were supposed to fall when he laid hands on us. After I finished laughing, I told her, "No." I knew what we were witnessing was real, but I'd never experienced it. I went up to sow my seed. As I got to the altar, the pastor called me out of line. He prophesied to me with a word of knowledge. There was no way he could know these things about me. He then laid hands on me. I remember a weight on my chest and down I went. I felt that peace again. This time, I understood that it was God all along.

I rededicated my life back to Christ and desired to learn more about Him. I enrolled in Catechism classes that were nine months long. I received answers to questions about God that I had long ago as a child in Baptist church. I chased after God more. I was hungry for Him. On February 14th, the pastor taught about the love of God. I began to see that I placed the men who I had been in relationships with before God. I wept all the way home. I repented and asked God to forgive me. I supported the needs of my husband. I ordered secure packs," which is packages sent to prisoners from their loved ones that consist of food, clothing and hygiene products. I drove two hours away on Saturdays to spend the day with him until visiting hours were over, then drove two hours back home. I prayed for him. I fasted and consecrated myself on his behalf.

At one point, my mom fell seriously ill and had to be hospitalized. I was constantly under emotional strain. The days became a constant blur. Some mornings were spent in the courtroom entangled in legal battles with my husband. My afternoons were consumed with responsibilities at work. Evenings were spent visiting my mother in the hospital and raising my children. There was no time to slow down and focus on my emotional health. Nor did I realize that I needed to.

My mom soon passed away. I felt like I didn't know how to live in a world without her. I remembered when I had suicidal thoughts and felt that my children would be better without me. I repented to God for wanting to stop living. Grieving and supporting a husband in prison was more than I could manage. I gave all that I had to my husband and didn't have any more to give.

That marriage ended in divorce. Here I was again, failing in yet another relationship.

My coworker asked me one day randomly if I wanted to begin dating. My response was, "I want to embrace where God is taking me." My daughter picked me up from work

I sang to God because I wanted Him to know that I loved Him, that I adored Him, that I belong to Him.

that day. As she drove, I cried, unbeknownst to her. I couldn't wait to get home and get in the presence of God. I closed my bedroom door, turned on worship music and began to sing to God as if my life depended on it. I sang to God because I wanted Him to know that I loved Him, that I adored Him, that I belong to Him. Whatever He wanted me to do, my answer was, "Yes!"

God began to download a book to me. I began to write. At that moment, I understood how the Bible was written by the inspiration of Holy Spirit. God gave me the outline for a book that I would later write. He gave me dreams. One night, I woke up and began writing what would be the strategy for my cheesecake bakery. He gave me the flavors of the cheesecake, the design of the business card, and even told me to make it an online cheesecake bakery. I had never heard of an online bakery. He led me to follow a woman on social media who taught about online business and marketing.

Years later, my ex-husband called me from prison. He was soon to be released. He spent ten years behind bars for what I continued to think were false charges. We talked about remarrying after his release. We set the date and even began to plan the wedding. Our relationship was rocky, but forward I marched. I ignored red flags in hopes of things settling down. It was difficult to communicate with him. It felt like he put up a wall every time I tried to discuss things. I didn't understand why this was happening. God showed me that he was bound. Deciding where to live after we were married was yet another argument. I wanted us to move into our own place. He wanted to live in his grandparents' house with his family. This was another strain on our relationship.

We got married on his grandparents' anniversary, at his request. I compromised and moved into his grandparents' home with the understanding that we would move as soon as we were financially able to move. The week after we got married was the last week he worked. Again, I found myself in a relationship where I carried the financial weight of the household.

I found a condominium for rent. We were set to move in at the beginning of November, two months after we were married. On moving day, my husband rented a U-Haul and moved all of *his* belongings into the condominium. It was the middle of December when my daughter's boyfriend, with the assistance of my husband, moved *my* belongings into the condominium. I prayed and asked God for a strategy for passive income. He said, "Digital products." I researched digital products and landed on creating an online course. We received a call from my husband's uncle who told us about a business conference happening in North Carolina in February. I sensed that God had something for me there. I did not know what. We were struggling financially, even though my husband found a job. I continued to carry the weight of the household bills. We made it to North Carolina despite our financial woes. God led me there to learn about speaking, creating a voice for my brand, and creating offers. While there, I met a woman of God. I'll share the significance of this meeting later. Armed with a new game plan, I returned home.

At the beginning of March, just under six months of marriage, I found out that my husband was cheating on me. My first response was to call my uncle to pray. That prayer saved me!

I moved all my belongings, changed my address, and filed for divorce within two weeks of me finding out that my husband deceived me. I woke up one morning disoriented. Initially, I didn't know where I was. Things happened so fast. I was completely broken. I could no longer take the pain. I couldn't keep pushing it deep down and keep it moving. I could no longer disguise what was going on internally. The pain and anguish I felt for allowing someone into my life, and the lives of my family, who ended up hurting, not only me, but my family, was unbearable. I knew I had to forgive him. I prayed and asked God to help me forgive him and to help my family forgive him. It did not happen overnight. Everywhere I went, I was triggered. I never experienced panic attacks or anxiety, but I was experiencing it after this.

My thoughts were consumed by conversations, memories and feelings. It was too much to manage on my own. It was difficult for me to get up out of the bed to get dressed. My feelings were not about missing him; they were about the pain he'd caused my family. I did not focus on the pain he caused me. I knew I needed to talk to someone. I visited a website that had multiple therapists I could choose. I prayed and asked God to lead me.

My first visit was online. In fact, *all* my visits were online, which made it convenient. During our first visit, my therapist asked me about my background. I shared with her what I did for a living and that I am also a pastor. She shared with me that she is an elder and we realized her son attended the same church I was now attending. This made me feel comfortable with her. Our visits were safe spaces for me to share things with her I've never shared with anyone else, including being molested as a child. She not only counseled me, but at times, God gave her a word for me. I felt like God was taking me through a healing journey.

God soon connected me with women who were praying women. My friend, who read a Scripture during my wedding, was one of the first people God connected me with. She prayed for me when I couldn't pray for myself. God revealed through her that He was going to use what I went through to catapult me into my destiny. God revealed to me that He wanted me to speak, to author books, to coach and to create podcasts. He shifted me from running my online bakery to researching coaching and mentoring programs. I came across the social media page of the woman of God, who I'd met in North Carolina. I saw that she was a Master Coach. I was intrigued, so I went on her website to see how her program worked.

That night, I had a dream about the woman of God. The dream was in black and white, except for my journal. My favorite journal is purple. When I saw the journal in color in my dream, I knew that God was telling me that the woman of God was my mentor. Weeks later, she posted about the launch of her mentorship program. All the things God told me to do were the very things offered in the woman of God's program. I signed up, and it was phenomenal. The first thing she did was take us through deliverance. I got to a point in therapy where my therapist felt that I no longer needed weekly or bi-weekly sessions. She told me that I could just reach out to her whenever I needed.

One afternoon, I attended an event with my friend. As we drove to the venue, it looked familiar. We went inside and it hit me. I was there with my ex-husband for my graduation from an accounting program. Unlike all the other countless times, I had no triggers. I felt absolutely nothing. It wasn't a numb feeling; it was a feeling of being healed. It was in that

I thank God that I am healed, whole and set free!

moment that I knew God healed me! I sat there in the middle of the event, crying. I was so grateful to God for healing me of the trauma. Not only the trauma from my most recent marriage, but the trauma from my childhood. In the dream that I shared at the beginning where God brought me back to my childhood home, the water that was present was symbolic of Holy Spirit. He was showing me that He had been with me through it all! He revealed to me in that dream that I was scared to launch out into the deep because I was playing it safe by staying near the shore.

Arizona Roberts also represented Holy Spirit because He is my friend and comforter. He was there to comfort me because I felt overwhelmed and anxious by the large body of water. The small canoe represents how I felt about myself. I felt small, insignificant. He showed me that I was choosing relationships out of my brokenness. God had to take me through deliverance and heal me in His own way.

I am now in a healed place. I have forgiven my ex-husband, as well as myself, for all the bad decisions I made. I thank God that I am healed, whole and set free! Even at your lowest point, know that God is with you. You may not sense His presence, but He is there. His Word says He will never leave you nor forsake you. Trust Him and lean on Him. You may be in a dark space; however, that is not the end of your journey. This is just one chapter. God is as close to you as the breath you breathe. Even when you cannot pray for yourself, He hears your cry, and He collects your tears.

 *Reflection Questions*

1. *How has God spoken to you in your dreams that might represent aspects of your personal journey?*

_____

_____

_____

_____

2. *How has past trauma or difficult experiences influenced your current relationships and self-perception?*

_____

_____

_____

_____

3. *How has external support, such as therapy, community or faith contributed to your growth and recovery?*

_____

_____

_____

_____

4. *What have been the key moments or turning points in your journey toward healing and self-discovery?*

_____

_____

_____

_____

5. *What steps can you take now to further pursue your goals and dreams, drawing from the author's story of resilience and transformation?*

_____

_____

_____

_____

ABOUT THE AUTHOR

Nicole D. Shepherd

*N*icole D. Shepherd, known as the "goal-getter" in life and business coaching, empowers individuals and entrepreneurs on their path to success. Her journey is one of remarkable resilience, having once been homeless and starting her life from nothing with two children and one on the way. In addition to her triumphs, Nicole is also a pastor, bringing spiritual insight and leadership to her coaching practice. She is a certified life coach, renowned for her ability to inspire and motivate individuals to achieve their fullest potential. As a captivating keynote speaker and author, Nicole integrates her extensive training in life coaching to provide comprehensive guidance, helping individuals navigate their personal, spiritual and business journey. Her expertise in personal development and entrepreneurship positions her as a sought-after resource in the industry.

RELENTLESS

Pearl Smith

The enemy has been relentless, striving to divert me from my purpose since the very beginning—since the womb. Before I entered this world, and now as an older adult, his mission has been clear: to silence the Word of God that He intended to spread through me. There were moments when it seemed like the enemy might succeed. However, God, in His infinite wisdom and power, prevailed. All I can do is lift my hands in gratitude to God for the life I have been given. This life includes both blessings and challenges.

What a journey it has been, and what a journey it continues to be. I can sincerely say that I thank God for every ebb and flow, for every high and low that has marked my path—the past, the present, and all that is yet to come. This gratitude stems from a deep understanding of who God is and who I am in Him. I have learned the beauty and the strength that comes from surrendering voluntarily to God.

This surrender isn't born out of weakness, but out of a profound recognition of identity—knowing who I am and,

more importantly, *whose* I am. Trusting in
the journey, whether it be mine or yours,
means trusting in God's perfect plan and
His unwavering love.

My journey of abandonment began before I even took my first breath.

Not Good Enough

From my earliest memory, I recall the gnawing feeling of
not being good enough. My journey of abandonment began
before I even took my first breath. I was abandoned by my
father while still in the womb. It seemed like I was destined
to wrestle with the weight of not being good enough. My
foundation was laid on shaky ground, with an alcoholic and
drug-addicted father whose absence carved deep scars into
my soul.

Raised by a single teenage mother, I was left to find love,
nurture and guidance in a world that already seemed
determined to strip me of my worth. As if that wasn't
enough, Satan added more to the burden, heaping
insufficiencies upon me, amplifying every flaw and feeding
every insecurity. The attacks were relentless, designed to
break me and to convince me that I was destined to struggle
with inferiority.

In the mid-seventies, gym class was a mandatory part of
elementary school, and I loved it. Gym was always a blast
for me. We jumped rope, played dodgeball and softball, and

ran until we were out of breath. We even climbed ropes, though I never quite made it to the top. It was still fun to try. Sometimes, we had to sit on the gym floor in rows of three or four, with about five or six students in each row. We'd sit one behind the other, either listening to the teacher or a guest speaker, or waiting for our turn at the next activity.

I dreaded those moments when we had to sit in rows, especially if someone was sitting directly behind me. I had a bald spot on my head. To this day, I'm not sure why the hair was absent there. I've come to believe that my mom didn't know how to cover it up. Also, at that time, weaves weren't popular or readily available. It was something I was self-conscious about, and sitting in those rows made it hard to ignore.

During this era, in African American culture, hair was a source of pride. The longer the hair, the better. Many of my classmates had naturally long hair, or their mothers straightened their hair with a pressing comb or hot comb to make it longer and straighter. Some of my classmates also wore their natural hair in ponytails, braids or afros—but not me. I barely had enough hair to braid, and certainly not enough for an afro. While my classmates could sport two ponytails, French braids, or plaits, I had to settle for four to six braids or ponytails. My hair just wasn't long enough for anything else.

I'm not sure how I ended up with a bald spot. It could have been from sleeping without a scarf. It could have been due to the nature of my hair type, tight rubber bands, a pressing comb burn, or simply because my mother didn't know how to properly care for my hair. Either way, my hair became a source of deep insecurity. Each time someone sat behind me, the teasing started.

"You've got a bald spot!"

"Turn around, Baldy!"

I can't forget the cruel nickname, "Baldilocks"—which was a play on *Goldilocks and the Three Bears*. I felt so defeated. There was nothing I could do to change their perspective. In first grade, my worth, my value, seemed to be determined by my hair—or lack thereof.

I suppose if my father had been there to tell me I was beautiful, that my hair—or its length—didn't matter, maybe I would have been okay. Maybe I could have walked around with confidence. But sadly, that didn't happen. My insecurity about my hair has haunted me my entire life. For fifty-six years, I've struggled to accept that I'll never have long, flowing hair.

Not a day went by without some little boy trying to grab or touch my chest.

The next target the enemy used to bully me was my breasts. I started developing breasts in the third grade, and they weren't small. I had the biggest breasts of all the girls in my class. Once they started growing, they didn't stop. I hated bras. Back then, they were made with underwires that pinched my skin. I hated wearing bras so much that, in sixth grade, despite my mom's disapproval, I started going to school without one. I thought that if I didn't wear a bra, I might look smaller than I was. In hindsight, I now know that wasn't true.

Having large breasts in elementary and middle school was a difficult and painful experience. Not a day went by without some little boy trying to grab or touch my chest. As if that wasn't bad enough, my classmates teased me and called me names like "Dolly Parton." I knew Dolly Parton's name before I even knew what she looked like. When I finally saw a picture of her, I was horrified. It was deeply unsettling to realize that this was how my classmates—and men—saw me.

I felt embarrassed and ashamed of my breasts. No one in my family had breasts as large as mine, so I constantly felt out of place. I always wore oversized sweaters, avoiding tight shirts or anything that might draw attention to my chest. I even started wearing t-shirts under every shirt, thinking it would help make my breasts appear smaller. In middle school, when we were required to shower after gym class, I often waited until most of the other girls had finished before I took mine. I'd walk to the shower, covering my chest as much as I could. My insecurity and shame were so deep that I even struggled to undress in front of my husband on our honeymoon. I wish I could say that these feelings disappeared after I got married, but they didn't. The shame and insecurity about my breasts stayed with me.

Still Not Good Enough

March 4, 2024, will forever be etched in my memory. One moment, I was sitting in my office, laughing and joking with my staff. The next, I was engulfed in a whirlwind of confusion. Just the previous week, I had undergone a breast biopsy, and I was supposed to receive the results by the end of the week. When the week ended with no words, I convinced myself that no news was good news. A friend reassured me of this, and I let myself believe her.

Then, a practitioner from the organization I work for called. I answered the phone cheerfully, assuming it was just a social call, especially since she wasn't the one who had performed the biopsy.

But then she said, "Pearl, I have your results. They came back positive for breast cancer."

I was speechless.

I thought no news was good news. The reality of what she was saying felt surreal. Cancer didn't run in my family—certainly not breast cancer. I sat down at my desk and cried while my practitioner friend explained what my next steps would be.

I thought I hated my breasts before, but this brought on a whole new level of hatred.

My breasts, which had been the source of so much trauma in my childhood, were now trying to kill me. I thought I hated my breasts before, but this brought on a whole new level of hatred. I felt utterly defeated as I sat there, crying at my desk, listening to my friend on the other end of the line.

I scheduled an appointment to meet with a team that included a surgeon, oncologist and radiologist. At this point, my cancer was classified as Stage 1. Surgery and radiation were the recommended treatments. I was given the choice between a lumpectomy, or mastectomy. My surgeon also added that my insurance covered a breast reduction if I wanted reconstructive surgery. Despite my long-standing hatred of my breasts, the thought of losing them was overwhelming. These breasts, which had been a source of insecurity, were also responsible for feeding my children— a redeeming quality that made the idea of parting with them deeply sad. In the end, I chose the lumpectomy, which meant I would need radiation and hormone therapy since I had not completely gone through menopause. Everything was happening so quickly, but I convinced myself that I could handle it.

I completed the surgery and had the lump removed, along with some lymph nodes. Before scheduling radiation, I needed to meet with the oncologist for the final lumpectomy results. Once again, I was having a good day when my oncologist called.

"Pearl, your results are back. Your type of breast cancer is hormone-driven, and it's now at stage 2. The best course of treatment for this type of breast cancer is chemotherapy, followed by radiation."

This call was even more traumatizing than the initial diagnosis of breast cancer. The thought of toxic chemicals flowing through my body, eradicating not just cancer cells, but also some of my healthy cells, terrified me. I was so afraid. My first thought was about my hair. It still wasn't that long, but the bald spot had long since disappeared. I was now wearing Sisterlocks, which allowed me to embrace my natural hair.

I remember the day I decided that I wanted to love my hair, to be okay with the hair God had given me. I had a perm at the time. One day, I looked in the mirror and saw the straightness of the perm against my curly roots. In that moment, I took a pair of scissors and cut off every bit of permed hair until I was left with a tiny afro. My new growth was substantial enough for me to two-strand twist my hair, which I wore until I decided to loc it. I decided on Sisterlocks because I wanted my locs to be small enough to style. Sisterlocks were a game changer for me. I often joked that I was having a love affair with my hair. But the truth was I loved my locs deeply. SisterLocs allowed my confidence with my hair to grow each day. Even when I had to cut them after dyeing them blonde and my hair started falling out, I still loved my locs. Embracing my natural hair had been a journey, and the idea of losing my tresses to chemotherapy was devastating. I silently heard the taunting and teasing of Baldilocks, and I became a young, insecure girl again.

When the oncologist told me I would need chemotherapy, I mourned the loss of my locs. I couldn't believe what the oncologist was telling me. I questioned her relentlessly: "Why couldn't you have told me this when you first discussed my stage? Why is chemotherapy necessary? What happens if I choose not to undergo chemotherapy?" I had so many concerns and questions that she asked me to come into her office for a face-to-face discussion. Even then, I struggled to accept what she was saying. She provided me with reading material about my type of cancer and scheduled a follow-up appointment to discuss my decision.

I was furious with God. I cried and screamed at Him, trying my best not to ask, "Why me?" even though I wanted to.

I was furious with God. I cried and screamed at Him, trying my best not to ask, "Why me?" even though I wanted to. It was so unfair. My belief is that you must accept both the good and the bad from God. I would be willing to do that if I didn't have to undergo chemotherapy. I realized I was conditional in my surrender to God's will for my life.

When I went to my appointment to talk with the oncologist, I hoped she would tell me there had been a mistake, that I had been given someone else's results, and that I wouldn't need chemotherapy after all. Unfortunately, that wasn't the case.

I still wasn't convinced that this was my fate. I cried a lot—not so much out of depression—but from disbelief. However, my oncologist was firm that I had breast cancer and that I had no choice but to accept my diagnosis. Accepting this diagnosis meant accepting that it was part of God's plan for my life. Once again, I had to come to terms with both the good and the bad from God, trusting that He could use both for His glory.

This story isn't just about the relentless teasing I endured as a child or my experience with breast cancer. This story is much deeper and bigger than either of those things. This story, no, this testimony, is about how God has helped me overcome the sources of trauma that have contributed to my insecurity for most of my life: abandonment, my hair and my breasts.

One of my favorite scriptures is Jeremiah 29:11-14a (NIV), which reads: *"For I know the plans I have for you, declares the Lord, plans to prosper you and not to harm you, plans to give you a hope and a future. Then you will call on me and come and pray to me, and I will listen to you. You will seek me and find me when you seek me with all your heart. I will be found by you, declares the Lord, and will bring you back from captivity."*

Trust the Plans of God

I often ask myself what it truly means to trust in God's plans. This is a challenging question because, as humans,

> *With God, things are different. ... He simply asks us to trust Him.*

many of us want to know everything that will happen or is supposed to happen in our lives. We want to know if we will get the job before the recruiter or employer calls us. We want to know what our unborn child will be, what will be at the potluck, who will be at the wedding, and how much something will cost—all before deciding. With God, things are different. We don't know His plans or how things will turn out, and He doesn't always reveal this to us. He simply asks us to trust Him. In my life, and perhaps in yours as well, we often have to move forward without knowing where we're going or what lies ahead.

I am reminded of a time when I was terminated from a position I had held for over ten years. This termination, which may or may not have been justified, came during a period when my mother was ill with cancer. As a District Manager, it was challenging to concentrate and perform my job while also trying to take care of and spend time with my mother, who had been given only months to live. I was struggling to balance my work responsibilities with caring for her. Eventually, I was let go. It was a bittersweet moment. I went on to care for my mother, who passed away just three months later.

A few weeks after my mom's funeral, my former employer called to check on me. I could almost hear my mom sternly encouraging that it was time to go back to work. To my surprise, my employer asked if I would come back. At that moment, returning to that place of employment was far from my intention. After all, they had fired me during one of the most challenging times of my life, leaving me feeling humiliated and embarrassed. I told her I needed to think about it. There were many factors to consider before I could decide whether to return to this organization.

I prayed to my Father, struggling to understand why He would send me back to that place. I thought about Moses and others in the Bible who were sent back despite their pasts. Moses had killed an Egyptian while trying to protect an Israelite. Pharaoh discovered this and sought to kill Moses, forcing him to flee. After several years, God got Moses' attention through a burning bush. He told Moses He had heard the cries of His people, and that Moses needed to return to rescue them. Moses questioned God's decision, expressing doubts. *"Why me? I'm not capable. Do you know who I am? I can't speak well. I'm not a leader. What if they remember my past and how I fled? I'm not a good example. The people won't follow me."*

Returning to that place didn't make sense to me, but it made sense to God. I asked Him to make it clear if this was what He wanted me to do. Though I was running out of money, I didn't want to take a job out of desperation. God made His will clear, and I chose to be obedient. Despite feeling embarrassed and uncertain about how the staff would perceive my return, I trusted in God's plan for my life. I went back.

While there, I cared for a patient who had led a difficult life and was searching for purpose. I shared the Gospel with him, explaining that God still wanted to use him. I believe that God can use all of us, with all that we have to offer, for His good—both the good and the bad. As humans, we must recognize that everything about us is valuable to God and can be used for His purpose. This patient later decided to follow God and now uses his life experiences to inspire others to trust in Him.

Shortly after this gentleman's conversion, I was moved to another part of the organization. My return was for this man's benefit. Just as Moses was sent to rescue the Israelites and show them a better way to demonstrate that God had heard their cries, I was sent to show this gentleman a better way and that God had heard his cries. I shudder to imagine what would have become of Moses' testimony had he not trusted God's plan and went back to save the Israelites, or what would have come of that gentleman God sent me to share the Gospel.

Trusting requires surrendering and leaving our feelings, insecurities and our desire to know behind.

We don't have to understand what God is asking of us. Trusting requires surrendering and leaving our feelings, insecurities and our desire to know behind. Trusting God also requires us to be okay with His plan. I have learned to be okay with short hair, no hair, breast cancer, loss and even abandonment.

Trust Who God Says You Are

In my role as a leader, part of my responsibility is to recognize both the strengths and weaknesses of my team members. When I notice a weakness, especially in someone who seems defensive or overly concerned with proving themselves, I often ask them, "Who told you that you weren't good enough?" I've observed that when someone is quick to defend themselves, or they insist on being right or perfect, it often stems from a deep-seated belief of inadequacy from childhood. I can recognize this because I wore that same badge. I constantly sought to prove my worth. I felt like being anything less than perfect was a personal failure.

The thought of falling short actually triggered anxiety and fear. I feared being fired, disliked or abandoned. Negative words from my childhood resonated louder than any positive affirmations. I believed that others were deserving of acceptance, but I was not. As I grew older, I realized that many people share these feelings of inadequacy. Understanding this has helped me approach my team with empathy and support.

Many times, we trust what God says about others, but we struggle to trust what He says about us. We show up for others, but we neglect ourselves. Why wouldn't we show up for ourselves? If we do some soul searching or self-assessment, and if we are honest, we may find that we don't believe we are valuable. We often hold onto others' perceptions of who we are. Some people view us positively, while others hold negative opinions. Unfortunately, we tend to give more weight to the negative views, and this is where we get stuck. I was stuck for years, feeling ugly and inadequate. I was labeled as "Baldilocks" or "Dolly Parton."

When I started losing my hair to chemotherapy, I was forced to confront myself honestly. I made the most courageous and frightening decision to let the strands fall naturally. I chose not to cut my hair. I watched each loc fall out one by one. After the last loc fell, I looked at myself in the mirror. No hair. No makeup. Just me. All of me. I cried, not because I thought I was ugly, but because everything I used to present myself to the world as worthy was gone. I was completely vulnerable, not only to myself, but to the world. I decided not to wear a wig or hair wraps. I wanted to present my true self to the world. God was teaching me to see myself as He sees me: beautiful, fearless, brave, courageous, valued and good enough.

Be brave enough to see yourself clearly and show up as your true, authentic self.

I encourage you to embrace your authentic self, scars and imperfections included. Be brave enough to see yourself clearly and show up as your true, authentic self. Understand that Satan does not want you to recognize the value in your scars and experiences. My father leaving me, my mother being a teenage mom, my short hair, and even having breast cancer were all part of God's plan for my life. The real question is this: Why does Satan want to keep us from understanding our value?

Satan does not want you to realize the power in embracing who God says you are. When we understand and trust our identity in God's sight, we become immensely powerful and can fight back victoriously. Imagine the businesses that would be started, the books that would be written, the future generations that would be shaped, and the reduction in crime that would occur if we simply stopped letting our past and others' perceptions of us dictate our responses. Instead, if we turned to the Most High God, and responded according to His guidance, our world could be so much better. I decided to trust God's plan for my life. I decided to trust God's perception of me. I invite you to trust God's plan for your life and embrace His perception of you. For it's truly only His plan and perception that truly matters.

Reflection Questions

1. *God's plans do not always make sense to us. Write about a time when trusting God did not make sense to you. What was the scenario and what was the end result?*

_____

_____

_____

_____

2. *What childhood perceptions about yourself are you holding onto that you need to let go?*

_____

_____

_____

_____

3. *You are powerful beyond what you can imagine. Satan understands how powerful you are. In what areas of your life is Satan stopping you from realizing your power?*

_____

_____

_____

_____

4. *You are valuable to God, scars and all. How can you use your scars to give God glory?*

_____

_____

_____

_____

ABOUT THE AUTHOR

Pearl Smith

*W*hile many people choose to march to the beat of their own drum, she understands that, without the support of others, that beat is incomplete. For Pearline Smith, author and motivational speaker, her passion for helping women see themselves as God sees them—and fully become that woman—makes her a magnet for those who need help, hope and healing. Affectionately known by many as simply Pearl, her pearls of wisdom and knowledge usher others into a life of fulfillment and wholeness—allowing them to become the gem they were originally intended to be.

As a great observer, keen listener and encourager, many people mistake this "quiet storm's" meekness for weakness. However, it's anything but. As a healthcare worker by trade, her innate ability to care for others, coupled with her passionate patience, positions her as a highly sought-after professional across multiple industries. A creative storyteller in her own right, Pearl is intentional about not just meeting new people but learning more about their personal journey. From failures and successes to disappointments and dreams, she speaks to everyone she encounters right at the point of their need—reassuring them that God has not left them and that He has a greater plan at work than what meets the eye.

While many women fight and belittle their way to the top, she argues that instead of We ascend higher faster when we collaborate, not compete.

Having published her first book, *Walking to the Beat of My Own Voice* in 2018, Pearl continues to empower women through her messages of triumph after tragedy. Contributing author of *From Fatherless to Fearless II* and *Recrowning God's Daughter II* Pearl is committed to letting women know she understands their struggles of not having an earthly father's validation. She strives to encourage women to know and to embrace their Heavenly Father who validation unconditional. Whether you've encountered her one time, or too many times to count, Pearl leaves a mark on the hearts and minds of others that cannot easily be erased—inspiring them to be the best version of themselves and to see the best in others.

For more information or booking, email pearldickerson@yahoo.com or call 248.514.3165.

THE PERFECT STORM A JOURNEY OF FAITH, STRENGTH & RENEWAL

Felecia R. Donald-Coleman

Storms are destined to happen to every one of us. When we're not equipped to handle various situations, unfortunately, they can be the breaking point for many. One thing I can say is that, as the Holy Spirit revealed so much to me in these last six years, I realize that God has always been with me in the storm. The enemy certainly created some storms to destroy me. God allowed some storms to make me into who He was trying to shape me to become. And some storms happened because of my personal choices.

Sometimes, we walk into situations with blinders, and we lack knowledge. I understand what the Bible says in Proverbs about getting an understanding in all our getting. I also understand when it says that we should lean on God and not on our own understanding. Some of the storms I encountered were because of wrong teachings in the church—teachings that did not give me the tools I needed to be successful in many areas of my life … namely, Holy Spirit.

Being raised in a Baptist church, God exposed me to so many things that made me curious and yearn for more. However, we were not taught about the Holy Spirit. We were not taught about speaking in tongues. But I'm grateful to the Baptist church for my firm foundation. If we don't have a firm foundation, everything else is rocky. For the most part, I had a firm foundation. I learned how to study the Word of God in the Baptist church, and I learned how to teach the Word of God in the Baptist church. But I did not learn the power and authority

This was the first time that the doctors told the nurse who cared for everyone else that she would never be able to return to work.

that I had after the Holy Ghost had come upon me. So, the perfect storm shook me to my core. There were many small storms, like rain showers.

But in 2018, the final perfect storm took place in my life.

This last storm was very traumatic naturally; however, it caused a total transformation spiritually. It was not the first time I had lost a home. It was not the first time I had been divorced. It was not the first time I had lost a job. The funny thing is, before all of this happened, the Holy Spirit told me I would not be able to take credit for what was about to happen in my life. So, when I had a near-fatal accident on my way to work after getting divorced in 2017 and lost the home that I had spent half of my retirement on, I honestly thought that was the end for me.

This was the first time I had divorced, lost my home, lost my car, and was physically inflicted to the point that I had to have 24-hour care. This was the first time that the doctors told the nurse who cared for everyone else that she would never be able to return to work. They said I would never be able to finish the doctoral program in nursing that I was in, nor seminary. This was the first time all the elements of a perfect storm were present simultaneously.

In the past, I'd experienced different elements of a storm. But all of them were not present at the same time. But this time, everything lined up to create a perfect storm. This storm devastated me. One thing I had, even though there was some doubt initially, was my relationship with God. I had to remember Romans 8:28, which says, *And we know that all things work together for good to them that love God, to them who are the called according to his purpose.* I had to remember that I was a child of God, an heir, and a joint heir with Jesus. I had to remember the benefits of my relationship with Christ.

In 2016, we found out that our company was outsourcing our entire department. We fought tooth and nail to save our department, but to no avail. We could either start over with no seniority with the new company, or, if we had a bachelor's degree in nursing, we were lucky enough to go to the health department. Some of us went to the juvenile detention facility because those areas were not outsourced.

I was faced with adversity, and people constantly reminded me that I had taken someone else's job.

December 31 was my last day at the jail. January 1, I started a new journey at the health department. Having a bachelor's degree took me to the health department, where I was not well received because of my status at the jail. Someone was displaced because I took their position. I was faced with adversity, and people constantly reminded me that I had taken someone else's job. I was not welcome, but I had to make it home. I still had to pay my bills. I still had to live.

Despite the rejection I received, disparate treatment and heavier caseloads than everybody else, I stood my ground. I came in, did my job, and went home. The longer I stayed at the health department, the more I grew on people. They noticed my knowledge and abilities and welcomed me to the health department.

In 2016, I was also separated from my husband. In 2017, we got divorced in March. In 2017, I was awarded a house that was in foreclosure. I had an attorney who agreed to fight for me, but then backpedaled and said that he was not taking my case any further. He laughed, talked and socialized in the hallway with the other attorney. They came and gave me an ultimatum for my nearly $300,000 house. They wanted to give me a drop in the bucket to walk away. If I didn't accept it, they were still going to take the house.

I'd lost my job of nineteen years. I was divorced. Now, I was losing my home that I'd put half of my retirement into. Although I was heavily burdened, I continued to pray. I continued to go before the Lord. I continued to worship, and I continued to walk, even though I was heavy.

I was already in a doctoral program in nursing, and I was in seminary at Destiny School of Ministry. I was building myself spiritually. I remember the day that my divorce was final—or so I thought. I was so excited about getting back to myself that I said, "I am getting back to me."

The Holy Spirit asked, "And who are you?"

That's when I realized that, from my youth until that very moment, I had lost *myself*.

The perfect storm put me in a position where I was stuck. I couldn't do anything but look at my life and see where I was and see where I had come from. In April of 2018, I moved into my new home. In June, I had a near-fatal accident. Two and a half years of my life were taken from me after this accident. I could not work or drive because the doctors wouldn't release me. The reports from every doctor were bad. I had occupational therapy, physical therapy and speech therapy at my home. I saw the neurologist, the ortho doctor, and my primary care doctor. I had so many appointments that appointments became my life. A transportation company was at my home almost every day, taking me from appointment to appointment.

Every appointment, every week that I went into, I left with shocking news. When I first walked into physical therapy, they said my body was in such bad shape that they couldn't even do physical therapy. They started using ice and heat to try to get my body to calm down. They transitioned me, after several months, into water therapy. From water therapy they transferred me to regular physical therapy, but on a smaller scale. I had to see an ENT for fractured ear drums. I was also seeing a neuro-ophthalmologist for fractured eyelids, blocked vision and damage to my eyes. When I tell you that everything lined up for me to quit ... but I refused.

Every appointment, every week that I went into, I left with shocking news. I had a nurse who was supposed to advocate for me, but she did nothing. I had no income. None of my paperwork had been filled out. I could communicate, but what I thought I was communicating was not what I was communicating. I found out that I had symptoms of a stroke, even though I hadn't had a stroke. It was a brain injury, resulting in me having aphasia, which made it hard for me to find the right words and express myself.

I had to stop doing everything. I went from house to house with people caring for me. Finally, I was taken back to my own home because I was just devastated at how my life was turning out. This takes me back to when I was a youth. At sixteen, I was pregnant with my first child, which was a result of rape. I was sitting at my dad's house with the Bible, being led by the Holy Spirit—though I didn't know it then—to read Job and Daniel. I didn't understand what that meant for my life, but I do now.

Job showed me that my life was going to be a struggle. However, I soon learned that the struggles were not about me. They were about those who are going to be helped by the things that I overcame. Daniel showed me that I could hear God and that I was a seer. Daniel also showed me that if I just listened to what God said, and obeyed, my life would be different. But here I am, years later from that sixteen-year-old girl, just now understanding the spiritual piece. This is horrible.

My coach once asked me, "What does success look like to you?" This was in 2019 after my accident.

I said, "Success, to me, looks like fulfilling what God has called me to do."

In the eyes of man and society, I was already successful. I was a registered nurse. I was a supervisor, and I ran the whole facility by myself—along with the support and assistance of the staff that was assigned to me. We worked as a team. I had raised my children and, even though I had been divorced more than once, I was happy where I was in relationships. I had a home—a beautiful home that I had built—which was my dream from childhood. I had a car that ran well. I was healthy. I had no issues with my body.

Then, the storm came.

The Holy Spirit took me back to earlier times in my life, showing me where He had been with me the whole time. He was with me through every trauma, through every divorce, through rape, through domestic violence, through homelessness, through no jobs … through every storm. He had been there, and He was still there with me right now.

How could I take credit for overcoming the perfect storm when I couldn't even remember things and my memory was messed up? PTSD and all the other diagnoses I received said that I would not survive this. But unlike Peter, who walked out on the water, took his eyes off Jesus, and began to sink, I pressed into God. I cried out to God. I kept my eyes on Him. I cried out to Him, asking, "Was I really that bad? What did I do to deserve this?"

I heard God ask, "Whose report will you believe?"

Those words shook me. I had to come to grips with everything that I had experienced. I broke and wept like a baby. This was the breaking point of the perfect storm. This was the point where I transformed.

Every one of us will have our faith tested in some way at some point.

Life has a way of hitting us all hard. Life will hit you right in the gut when we least expect it. Day after day, managing life and responsibilities, doing it, and making it work, is what we pride ourselves on. Then, one day, everything that can go wrong seems to go wrong. The Word of God in 1 Peter 4:12 (AMP) says, *Beloved, do not be surprised at the fiery ordeal which is taking place to test you [that is, to test the quality of your faith], as though something strange or unusual were happening to you.*

Every one of us will have our faith tested in some way at some point. The Word tells us that it rains on the just, as well as the unjust (Matthew 5:45). Difficulties in this life are par for the course. I believe that *perfect storms*, like what I experienced, where every area of my life was colliding at the same time—are there to strengthen us, to catapult us, and to get us back on the right path.

I was raised to be independent, to do things on my own. I thought that was a strength for me. So, when the Holy Spirit told me, "This time, you won't be able to do this; you won't be able to take credit for this," I really didn't understand it. When I had the accident, He said, "This accident is saving your life." I really didn't get that either. The accident shifted my life and took me into a place I thought I would never be in—the lowest of low—the very same place where Job found himself.

I was in a place where I really didn't have anywhere to go. Everything was falling apart in every area of my life. But when I heard, "Whose report do you believe?" God showed me every part of my life from my youth.

When I reached my breaking point, the only voice I wanted to hear was the voice of God.

He told me, "That was me when you went through this. That was me when you went through that. That was me." I realized that I was never alone in any of it—that God was always with me. One of the things the enemy likes to do is to make us feel like we don't have anybody. He wants to make us feel like no one else cares. People lose hope and commit suicide because they feel like they have lost it all and don't have any way out. But I'm here to tell you that there is hope at the end of every storm.

When I reached my breaking point, the only voice I wanted to hear was the voice of God. He showed me who I was before the rape. He showed me who I was before the trauma changed me. The new me was on the horizon. My identity had always been tied to others. I was Sheila's sister. I was Val's sister. I was Lee's sister. I was Pastor Weems' daughter. I was Pint's daughter. I was never simply identified as *me*.

So, I took on what I called The Martha Syndrome. I was busy, task-oriented, distracted by what everyone else wanted, pleasing everybody else, doing things the way everybody else felt that they should be done, and yet losing sight of me. I hadn't even realized that I had lost myself.

Everything that I ever experienced in my life—the trauma of having an absent father, the scars from the abuse of domestic violence, the rapes, the rejection, the pain in my body, having no place to go, and not having any income—came crashing down on me like a tidal wave.

I was drowning.

And in that very moment that I was drowning, it was like Peter on the water when he asked Jesus to bid him to come, and he stepped out on the water. I stepped out on every word that I've ever read and studied in the Word of God. My faith increased to a whole new level. At this point, enough was enough. The storm had stripped away all the distractions and left me face to face with my pain. I could no longer cover it. I could no longer hide it.

The winds of change were not just about external circumstances; things inside of me had to shift, as well.

But it was time to be healed.

I could no longer let all the negative things that were said about me or that were done to me dictate my life. It was time for my spiritual woman to mature and become everything God had ordained me to be. In the midst of this perfect storm, I realized that something had to change. I could no longer carry the burdens of my past while trying to navigate the challenges of the present. It was time for the wind of the Holy Spirit to blow and change every part of my life. This required me to confront the very things that I feared most— all of my failures, my insecurities, and my deepest wounds. It meant stepping out of my comfort zone and facing the storm head-on.

I know you've heard of growing pains. Each step in this new process required me to be patient. One of the things I've learned in this process is that it took a long time for me to get to where I was, so I had to be patient and allow time to heal. But the good news is that my thought processes— the way I saw things and the way I processed things—were no longer the same. The winds of change were not just about external circumstances; things inside of me had to shift, as well. Once I got the things inside healed, the outside would line up.

From a nurse's perspective, wounds heal from the inside out, not the outside in. So, restoration for me had to begin on the inside and permeate to the outside. My heart had to be restored and renewed. My thinking, my mind, my thoughts—everything about me internally—had to be addressed first. When the Holy Spirit asked me, "Who am I?" I had to remember that I am a child of God. I am fearfully and wonderfully made. He created me in His image and His likeness. Regardless of what anybody else says, I am somebody, and I have something to offer to this world.

Many years before my perfect storm occurred, I became curious about spiritual healing. My church was using space at Evangel Christian Church, and I picked up some flyers. One of the flyers was on inner healing and deliverance. This was back in the '90s. I started going to the inner healing and deliverance sessions on Saturdays. I went through the inner healing and deliverance process, and I even ministered inner healing and deliverance, which I still do. But I had no idea that I was going to go to a whole new level of inner healing and deliverance during this storm. In order to come out of the storm, I had to find a place of refuge, a safe haven. That place was totally in God.

It was at this moment that I had to give God a real, "Yes." Matthew 11:29-30 says, *Take my yoke upon you, and learn of me; for I am meek and lowly in heart: and ye shall find rest*

unto your souls. For my yoke is easy, and my burden is light.
This came to life for me. I came to realize that inner healing
is not just a one-time thing; it's a continuous process. We
have to peel back layers of trauma, layers of hurt, layers of
disappointment, and allow ourselves to be vulnerable and
open to what God wants to do in our lives.

It's going to be difficult, but God wants to heal us
everywhere we hurt. God wants us healed. He wants us
whole. The Word of God says, I would that you prosper and
be in health, even as your soul prospers. As we grow in Him,
we can be healed. As we let things die in us, we can be
healed. As we walk out of fear, we can be healed. Today, I
meditate on His Word. I worship more and pray more. I stay
in God's face. I stand firm on His Word.

You have to stand firm on His Word. The Bible says a
double-minded man is unstable in all his ways. If we're
unstable, our situations are going to be unstable. We must
be firm. Standing firm in the storm also means learning to
let go of control. I no longer had control. I had to surrender
my needs and everything about me to God and trust Him
to do it.

One of the most powerful lessons I learned during this
time was the importance of reclaiming my identity. I spent
so many years defining myself by what others needed me
to be, but I realized that my true identity wasn't tied to

You can't save anybody else if you haven't saved yourself first.

any of those things. It was rooted in God. He was the one who created me. I had to embrace who God said He made me to be and continue to stand firm on His Word.

You're going to have to let some things go. You're going to have to empty everything and allow God to rebuild. Rebuilding was not just about putting the pieces back together; it was about creating new and stronger things. The first person I had to forgive was myself. I was the first partaker of the rebuilding process.

You're no good to anybody else if you don't have yourself together. You can't save anybody else if you haven't saved yourself first. I had to work on me. The repairs began with me. Every time I wanted to give up, I was reminded of God's promises in Isaiah 61:3, that He would bestow on them a crown of beauty instead of ashes, the oil of joy instead of mourning, and a garment of praise instead of a spirit of despair. This promise gave me hope. It reminded me that God was in the business of restoration and that He could take the broken pieces of my life and create something beautiful.

Now, I'm on a new horizon. Today, I can see how the storm was absolutely necessary. It was painful, but it purged me. It stripped me. It purified me. It removed everything that would hinder me from the next place that God was taking me. The storm forced me to deal with my past traumas and the wounds. I learned to set boundaries, understanding that setting boundaries did not mean that I had to cut off people. I had to cut off things that would prevent me from growing and allow myself the space to heal. As I move forward, I do so with a sense of peace, knowing that I have been through the storm and come out on the other side.

I do understand as a child of God that storms are unpredictable. When the storm comes, and sometimes it rages, I am stronger in rising and more resilient because of it. I will continue to stand firm in my faith and remain anchored and confident in my identity.

I had to find faith, and I had to learn that courage did not mean that fear was not present. Courage, which would give me faith, was a decision that I had to make to trust God regardless of what was going on around me and to know that He's got it all in control.

I also learned that faith required me to do something. Faith requires action, especially in the storm. I had to decide every day to stand on God and the Word. I had to decide every day to trust in Him, spending all the time that I could in prayer, even when I didn't feel like it. I spoke God's promises over my life, speaking the Word of God that gives life, even when my circumstances looked different. We walk by faith and not by sight. Without faith, it's impossible to please God. Faith doesn't make the storm disappear. It gives us strength to endure. It anchors us. Storms don't leave us the same. They strip away the things we thought we needed, and they reveal the things that truly matter.

Reclaim yourself and reclaim your identity. It's a daily decision to choose truth over lies, faith over fear, and love over rejection. Replace the lies with the truth, which is God's Word. The truth will make you free. It's a process of unlearning the things the world has taught you about yourself and embracing the truth of who God says you are. For me, this process involved practical steps like journaling, prayer, meditation, singing, music and worship. Lean on God. He is the author and finisher of your faith. There is life beyond the storm. Be resilient. Be adaptable. Maintain your healing and get around others who are healed.

Here a few tips to remember:

1. **Reaffirm your identity in Christ.** Remind yourself daily of who you are in Christ. Meditate on Scriptures like Psalm 139:14 and 2 Corinthians 5:17 to solidify your divine identity.

2. **Practice forgiveness and inner healing.** Forgiveness is key to healing from trauma, including forgiving yourself. Release past hurts to God, and allow Him to heal your wounds, forgiving others and yourself

(Ephesians 4:32). Self-forgiveness is essential for inner healing and growth.

3. **Build a supportive community.** Engage with a faith-based community for support and encouragement (Ecclesiastes 4:9-10).

 *Reflection Questions*

1. *How has your past influenced how you see yourself?*

   _____

   _____

   _____

2. *What steps can you take to rediscover your authentic identity?*

   _____

   _____

   _____

3. *List the areas in your life where you still hold onto hurt and unforgiveness. Include names of the individuals, the incidents and how it made you feel.*

   _____

   _____

   _____

4. *How would letting go of those painful emotions help you to heal and gain peace?*

_____

_____

_____

5. *Visualize yourself in the middle of a storm! How would fully trusting God help you through this storm?*

_____

_____

_____

ABOUT THE AUTHOR

Felecia R. Donald-Coleman

*F*elecia R. Donald-Coleman is fondly known as Coach Fee to some and Mama to many. A dedicated leader and healer, she has worked for 40 years in healthcare, with 34 years as a registered nurse (RN), specializing in women's and infants' health, public health and correctional healthcare. She also has experience in utilization review, ensuring effective use of medical resources.

Felecia played a key role in opening the pediatric unit at Grace Hospital and developing the Crisis Management Unit (CMU) in a correctional facility. As an ordained apostle and chaplain, she ministers inner healing and deliverance, helping others overcome trauma, fear and self-limiting beliefs. As the founder and CEO of Sisters Invoking Success, REdefining Self Coaching and Consulting, and Donald-Coleman Enterprises, Felecia empowers underserved communities through trauma recovery, financial literacy and specialized services. Her work is driven by a deep commitment to building a lasting legacy of service and empowerment.

Felecia has overcome significant personal challenges, including an absent father, divorce, surviving rape, situational homelessness, and self-limiting beliefs. These experiences fuel her passion for helping others reclaim their self-worth. Felecia is a contributing author in the anthology, *Take the Limits Off*. She hosts the podcast, REdefining Self w/Coach Fee, which focuses on overcoming fear and self-limiting beliefs using biblical principles, and includes weekly Sunday school lessons.

Felecia currently works as a substitute teacher and has a passion for teaching grades Pre-K through eighth, especially Pre-K and Kindergarten. Felecia's unwavering commitment to healing, empowerment, and service continues to inspire and uplift countless lives, ensuring her legacy of love and transformation endures. Schedule your free consultation today with REdefining Self Coaching and Consulting for a transformational journey at https://linktr.ee/1coachfee!

HOW THE ENEMY TRIED TO TAKE ME OUT

Arleen Young

I am the oldest of five siblings. I was born and raised in the cities of Detroit and Hamtramck, Michigan. I developed a condition as a newborn where I couldn't keep milk down. Every time my mom fed me, I threw up. When I was only two days old, I had to have an operation. I had to get my hair shaved. I had needles in my head for an IV, and I was cut open to save my life. After I was in the recovery room, no one monitored me. I kept moving and squirming until I rubbed a big hole in my right wrist. It scarred me for life. People often asked if I tried to commit suicide. The enemy wanted to take me out!

As a young child, I saw and heard some things that no child my age should have. I saw domestic violence. I saw people drinking liquor, cussing, fighting. A family member touched me sexually in the sixties, but I never told anyone. I told my mother when I was well into my forties. I carried this pain and shame for many years. This was the beginning of fear. The enemy tried to destroy me with fear. It was so bad that I thought about taking my life. I became paranoid of people. I always thought people were out to get me. I felt like no one loved me. I was always defending myself because that was my only mechanism to protect myself. The enemy had me thinking I was worthless, ugly and crazy. He made me believe that no one cared for me.

However, I knew it was something deeper that was destroying my soul.

Fear is a real emotion I've carried for over forty years.

When I was growing up, I always loved to write poetry and read. Reading and writing were my passions. They were my getaways from the real world. I was always book smart, but I lacked common sense. I also lacked social skills because of fear. Socially, I had a terrible sense of being shy. I could not look people in the eyes because I was scared. Don't get me wrong. I was raised by a good mom because my father was not in the home.

My mother took care of me and my siblings very well. However, I knew it was something deeper that was destroying my soul. So, I started buying things and I kept them in my room. My stepfather and my mother operated a party store in the late seventies and early eighties. I would take things like candy, cigarettes, beer, wine, chips and lotion from the store. These things made me feel good. I was in control. I owned something. That alone made me feel good.

One day, my mother came in my room and saw over 50% of her store in my bedroom. That's when the hoarding began. My mother made me put every item I took back to the store. But that didn't stop me from hoarding. I bought many things I did not need. I even bought things just because I had the money. I had it bad. When I finally moved out of my parents' home, the hoarding never stopped. I collected books, clothes, jewelry and even food. Thrift stores were my number one stores.

No one ever told me this was a mental condition. If I didn't have things, fear would take over me. People loved me, but they speculated about my horrible weakness. I did not trust anyone. I missed family engagements and parties because of fear. When I did go to gatherings, I hid in the bathroom. I wanted to be nowhere in sight. This worried my mother. She always instilled in me that I was smart, pretty and outgoing. My mother told me I could be anything I wanted to be. I just didn't believe it. Many other people talked down to me. When I did speak up for myself, I was already labeled as a troublemaker. I always started stuff or caused confusion. I accepted it. I was full of fear and shyness. Many people took this weakness for granted. I knew I had to take matters into my own hands. I went to a doctor and told her everything.

The doctor prescribed medication for me. My mother thought it might be a good idea, but I refused to take it. Fear was a natural mechanism of my life. I functioned

I lived an unsaved life until my forties.

alright; I had a few friends. I graduated from high school and college. I always had a decent job. I was the first to graduate from college among my siblings, but fear was yet hidden inside me.

I grew up in church. My mom and grandmother made sure me and my siblings were in church every Sunday. They made sure we attended Sunday School. As I continued to go to church, I really found out that fear came straight from the devil. The devil comes to steal, kill and destroy. I really got scared because I thought, "Am I a devil's child?" I was in and out of church in my younger years.

I've dated and went to parties, but I was only *truly* in love with two men in my life: my children's father and my high school sweetheart. God bless their souls. They are now deceased. This also drew fear in me.

I lived an unsaved life until my forties. Then, one day I rededicated my life back to Jesus Christ—only to go back out in the world and do what I wanted. My mother was a woman of God. She always prayed continuously for our family. Even when me and my siblings came to visit my mother, she never let us depart without praying. I knew prayer was powerful, but I always depended on my mother's prayers. I depended on her to lead prayer. I didn't have prayers of my own. My mother prayed us out of trouble many times.

One day, I called my mother early one morning while I was going to work. I wanted her to pray for me about a specific situation that was going on at work She told me, "Look, Arleen. I am sleepy. But I will agree with you now. Pray or I am going back to bed."

I said, "Mom! Mom, you have always prayed and could get a prayer through!"

Silence was on the phone. She waited until I started praying. Once I did, she agreed with me and said, "Have a blessed day!"

I was mad. Little did I know, God was up to something. So, as I visited my mother, she always asked me to lead prayer. I wanted to pray, but I did not want to lead prayer. She would not start prayer until I led prayer with my family. I did not want to disrespect God. I did not know any better until 2013 when God brought me out of some things that I know could have, should have and would have taken me out! In 2013, I rededicated my life to the Lord Jesus Christ and became a prayer warrior for Jesus Christ. I prayed for people on my job, my friends, my children and my family. When I prayed, things happened. That is when fear began to leave my life, slowly but surely. God gave me the gift of becoming a prayer warrior. It was my only weapon that could fight the demons associated with my fear. He was preparing me to fight the enemy.

Today, I pray the following with authority from God's Holy Word:

1. No weapon that is formed against me shall prosper.

2. Submit to God. Resist the devil and he will flee.

3. Greater is He that is in me than he that is in the world.

4. For God so loved the world that He gave His only begotten Son.

5. Where there are two or three gathered in Jesus' name, He is in the midst.

God showed me who He was. He is the Alpha and Omega, the beginning and the end. So, as I was getting stronger in my prayer life, I prayed with my prayer partner. I've known her for many years since middle school. We pray at the same time every day to fight the enemy. I have learned to get back, stand still and let God! For God has not given me the spirit of fear, but of love, power and a sound mind. I am still human and have obstacles. God is still dealing with me. I am not like I used to be, and I sure do not look like what I have been through. I made a few alignments, but that comes with age.

Prayer defeated my fear that I carried for many years.

God is a way maker. God is the truth and the light. He is powerful. To get to Him, you must go through our Lord and Savior, Jesus Christ. Prayer defeated my fear that I carried for many years. After I became a prayer warrior, God showed me who He is and that I can totally trust Him. One time, my son's wife was looking for him because she was running late for work. She called everyone, asking if they had seen him. I told her to keep calling. I knew he would pick up eventually. When he did pick up, he said he got pulled over by the police. Then, the phone went dead. My daughter-in-law was a nervous wreck. I started calling on the name of Jesus. I called my prayer partner. We prayed and demanded the enemy to let him go. Come to find out, he was on the other side of town, visiting a friend to estimate a car repair job. The police pulled my son over because they detected there was no insurance, and he had some outstanding traffic tickets.

So, they handcuffed him and prepared to take him to the police station. Out of nowhere, the police officers got a call saying there was an active robbery going on not even a block away. They looked at my son, uncuffed him, gave him back his keys, and told him to leave and straighten out his business. He came riding down the street, honking the horn and shouting, "The police were about to take me to jail, and they let me go!" I just started shouting, "Lord! You are faithful!" He heard my prayers. He heard my prayer partner's prayers.

Another praise report was when my oldest daughter was coming home from high school. One afternoon, she walked upon a pack of ten dogs. She just froze. If she would have taken off running, they were going to chase her. I pray for my family every day when nothing is wrong. I knew my daughter was scared for her life because dogs can be vicious. Out of nowhere, a woman came out and directed all those dogs toward her. My daughter was free to go. Praise God! You cannot tell me God is not good. He may not come when we want, but He is sure on time. Prayer works. It melts God's heart when we pray.

I tell my family all the time that we are not exempt of this world. However, when you put God first, things happen in your favor.

Another time, I was extremely ill. I had pain in my stomach on one side. I thought it was something I ate. Maybe I'd pulled a muscle. I didn't go to work that day. thought Tylenol would take it away. I was telling a friend about it, and she urged me to go to the hospital. The ER took me right away and said if I would have waited another hour, I would have died. My appendix was about to burst. But God!

My mother had to get my kids from school while I was on the operating table. It's nothing but the grace and mercy that God spared my life. I prayed while on that operating table before I was knocked out. I tell my family all the time that we are not exempt of this world. However, when you put God first, things happen in your favor. If I continued to be afraid like the enemy wanted me to be, I would not have conquered the battles I faced. I am not a preacher or prophetess. I'm simply a messenger of God, telling my story. God also saved my dear mother from a terrible accident on 1-94 while she was taking my brother to the airport.

She was on her way back after dropping him off. A semi-truck jumped in front of her, and she knew she was going to die. The car turned all the way around and the truck smashed her car to pieces. My sister said my mother should have been dead based on how the car looked. I was a nervous wreck. Jesus reminded me that He's got her. I have so many more stories on how God brought me and my family out. I let fear, the enemy's biggest weapon, keep me down. But now I'm free.

I still have my moments when I need to just meditate and talked to God. I thank Him for bringing me out. I want you to become stronger. Let go and let God. I hope this has helped you in knowing that, if God did it for me, He can do it for you. Ask God to take you higher in Him.

In order to please God, you have to be consistent. We cannot pray on Monday and pray later on Thursday. That's not how it works. It would be wonderful to make a war room (prayer room) in your house where you have a dedicated time with just you and Jesus. You have to pray *every day*. Morning, noon and night. Pray over some oil, anoint your house and watch God.

Get in a Bible-based church that will teach you truth. Read your Bible daily. God's Word is our spiritual food. The enemy cannot stand up against God's Word. He will flee and try to use someone close to you. The enemy is always on his job. We have to be on ours. Prayer can defeat anything! Jesus may not come when you want Him to, but He is always right on time.

 *Reflection Questions*

1. *How often do you pray to God and how can you increase your prayer time?*

_____

_____

_____

2. *How do you handle situations that are not in your favor?*

_____

_____

_____

3. *What do you maintain your faith in the midst of fear?*

_____

_____

_____

4. *What other things have you put before God?*

_____

_____

_____

5. *How can you better practice being a doer of the Word of God and not just a hearer?*

_____

_____

_____

ABOUT THE AUTHOR

Arleen Young

*A*rleen Young has always had a passion for reading and writing. She always dreamed of becoming an author. Arleen has shown leadership, ambition and a unique gift of writing poetry. Realizing that she could think of something from the top of her head and draft a poem within minutes, she started her trend of writing poems for her grandchildren. With her innate ability and love for reading and writing, God took her down the path of teaching.

Arleen has been a teacher for twenty-three years. She has touched many lives, young and old. She has taught: ELA, Spanish, Biology, Physical Science, Chemistry and Math. She holds a bachelor's in health administration from the University of Detroit Mercy and a Master of Art in Secondary Education Integrated Science from Wayne State University. Arleen has three grown children, eight grandchildren and one great-grandchild. For educational consultations or services, email SpeaktheTruth64@yahoo.com.

ABOUT

So It Is Written

We help Christian female speakers and coaches write the ONE book that will expand their reach and generate 7-12 streams of income in record time! Period!

As the leading content curators for six-figure authorpreneurs and entrepreneurs, So It Is Written is best known for helping them package and leverage their expertise into a bestselling book, which amplifies their brand, accelerates their paydays and attracts bigger opportunities!

Let us help you brand in excellence as an author and entrepreneur so you can develop multiple streams of income from just ONE book!

Call us at 313-777-8607 today or email info@soitiswritten.net for more details about our services. We look forward to collaborating with you to make your project one of excellence!